D0787662

HUMAN SACRIFICE

Gareth Stevens
Publishing

Alix Wood

Please visit our website, **www.garethstevens.com**. For a free color catalog of all our high-quality books, call toll free 1-800-542-2595 or fax 1-877-542-2596

Library of Congress Cataloging-in-Publication Data

Wood, Alix.
Human sacrifice / by Alix Wood.
  p. cm. — (Why'd they do that? strange customs of the past)
Includes index.
ISBN 978-1-4339-9585-9 (pbk.)
ISBN 978-1-4339-9586-6 (6-pack)
ISBN 978-1-4339-9584-2 (library binding) --
1. Rites and ceremonies—Juvenile literature. 2. Human sacrifice—Juvenile literature. I. Wood, Alix. II. Title.
GN473.W66 2014
390—dc23

First Edition

Published in 2014 by
Gareth Stevens Publishing
111 East 14th Street, Suite 349
New York, NY 10003

© Alix Wood Books

Produced for Gareth Stevens by Alix Wood Books
Designed and illustrated by Alix Wood
Picture and content research: Kevin Wood
Editor: Eloise Macgregor
Consultant: Rupert Matthews, the History Man

Photo credits:
Cover, 1, 4, 5, 6 left, 7 background and bottom left, 8 left, 9, 14, 15, 16, 17, 18 bottom, 22, 23 bottom, 25, 26 top, 27 top, 28, 29 © Shutterstock; 3 © British Museum, 6 right © Bruger, Malene/Moesgaardmuseum; 7 inset © Sven Rosborn; 8 right © Public Domain; 10 top © Luidger/National Museum of Anthropology; 12 top © Sean Pathasema/Birmingham Museum of Art; 12 bottom © Duncan Stonebridge; 13 main © iStock; 13 inset © Public Domain; 18 inset © Thomas Aleto; 19 bottom © Public Domain; 20 © Public Domain; 21 bottom © OCadena; 23 top © Rose Manios; 26 bottom © Public Domain

Printed in the United States of America

CPSIA compliance information: Batch #CS13GS: For further information contact Gareth Stevens, New York, New York at 1-800-542-2595.

Contents

What Is Human Sacrifice?

A sacrifice is the destruction of a thing to please the gods, spirits, or the dead. Human sacrifice is the act of killing one or more human beings as part of a religious **ritual**. The more valued the creature is that is sacrificed, the greater the honor believed to be given. The most valuable of all life is that of a human being, and human sacrifice was the greatest possible ritual gift.

Human sacrifice has been practiced in many cultures throughout history. Victims were typically ritually killed as an offering to please the gods. Sacrifices would often happen during times of **famine** or hardship, when it was thought the gods must be angry. Some sacrifices were done voluntarily by the victims. In some cultures, wives would throw themselves onto the funeral **pyres** of their husbands, or sometimes servants would kill themselves after the death of their master.

REALLY?

The practice of human sacrifice may have bonded a society together! It may have helped remove individuals that had a bad effect on the community, such as criminals, religious **heretics**, foreign slaves, or prisoners of war.

WHO WERE THEY?

Victims for sacrifice were usually taken from one of two very different categories. They would be chosen as a particularly pure or valuable human being, for instance a child, a young maiden, or a young warrior. Or they would be an outsider, a prisoner, someone from a defeated enemy, or a slave. Slaves might also be purchased specifically to be sacrificed, avoiding the need to kill a member of the community. However, when captives and slaves were in short supply, victims might be taken by force from among the community.

Sometimes an important person's servants were sacrificed so that they could serve their recently deceased master in the next life. In 537 BCE, the rulers of the Shang Dynasty in China were buried with the sacrificed bodies of their servants. Later in China's history, manpower was scarce and model figures of armies and servants were buried instead, like the 8,000 amazingly crafted terracotta warriors at the tomb of Qin Shi Huangdi (below).

Bog Bodies

Human sacrifice was practiced at least 5,000 years ago among the early agricultural societies of Europe. The cold peat bogs of northern Europe preserved the bodies so well that when some were found, people thought they had discovered a recent crime scene!

Three bog bodies were found in Britain dating from around 100 CE. The evidence points to them having been sacrificed. One man had been hit very hard on the head and his throat had been slit. A leather **garrotte**, tightened with a slipknot, was still around his neck. He was naked except for a fox-fur armband and in his stomach there was mistletoe pollen, a plant sacred to the Celts and Britons. One of the bodies had six fingers. Many bog bodies from northern Europe have physical defects and may have been selected for sacrifice because of their deformity.

REALLY?

Grauballe Man was uncovered in 1952 from a peat bog in Denmark. Judging by his wounds, he was killed by having his throat cut. Another preserved man and a woman were found nearby and also appear to have been sacrificed.

Grauballe Man

mistletoe

SACRIFICE OR MURDER?

Most bog bodies that have been discovered date from the Iron Age (1200 BCE – 400 CE), a time when peat bogs covered a large area of northern Europe. Many of these Iron Age bodies have a number of similarities, which make experts believe there was a cultural tradition of killing and depositing these people in a certain manner. For these people, the bogs held some sort of importance, and they placed offerings into them, perhaps to gods of fertility and good fortune. It is believed that the Iron Age bog bodies were thrown into the bog for similar reasons, and that they were therefore examples of human sacrifice to the gods. Many bog bodies show signs of being stabbed, bludgeoned, hanged or strangled, or a combination of these methods. Usually the corpses were naked. In a number of cases, twigs, sticks, or stones were placed on top of the body, sometimes in a cross formation, and at other times forked sticks were driven into the peat to hold the corpse down.

Tollund Man, from Denmark, was found with the rope used to strangle him still around his neck. His remains were found near those of Grauballe Man.

Layers of sphagnum moss and peat helped to preserve the bodies from **oxygenization**.

Ancient Americas

The ancient civilizations of the Americas are well known for their human sacrifices. Aztec priests believed that human sacrifices were necessary to keep the sun on its daily path. The Incas thought children sacrificed to the sun god brought prestige on the child's parents and their village. Mayans would sacrifice humans to celebrate a new leader or the completion of a temple.

The Aztecs believed that those who died in sacrifice would go to the paradise of the sun. A human sacrifice repaid the gods with the soul of a person. They believed this was necessary to keep the world from coming to an end. At some festivals, a person was chosen to represent a god. For the amount of time left before their sacrifice the person would dress, act, and be treated as the god they were representing. It was believed that at the point of sacrifice, the god actually entered the human representing them.

A map showing where the Aztecs, Mayans, and Incas lived

An Aztec sacrifice

MOUNTAIN MUMMIES

Mummies of sacrificed children have been found in the mountains of South America. The Incas performed child sacrifices for important events. Children were chosen as they were considered to be the purest of beings. Months before the sacrifice, the children were fattened up. They were dressed in fine clothing and jewelry and taken to Cuzco to meet the emperor. A feast was held in their honor. The Inca high priests took the victims to mountaintops for sacrifice. The journey was extremely long and breathing was difficult at such high altitude. They ate coca leaves to help them breathe and allow them to reach the burial site alive. Once there, the children were given an **intoxicating** drink and then killed either by strangulation, a blow to their head, or by leaving them to die of exposure.

The Andes mountains and the ruins of the ancient Inca city of Machu Picchu

REALLY?

The average age for an Inca child sacrifice was between 8 to 10 years old. The children were prepared, their hair was braided, and they were covered in delicately woven tapestry. The children usually came from noble families, and they were honored to be chosen for the sacrifice!

Aztec Sacrifices

During an Aztec sacrificial ritual, the victim would usually climb the temple steps and lie on a stone slab. He or she would be held down by four priests, while a fifth made an incision in the victim's abdomen with an **obsidian** knife. A second cut was made in the chest, and the victim's beating heart was ripped out and held towards the sky for the Sun-God.

This jaguar-shaped stone vessel was used to hold the hearts of sacrificed victims.

Tlaloc was the god of rain. The Aztecs believed that if child sacrifices weren't made for Tlaloc, rain wouldn't come and their crops would die. If the children cried on their way to their sacrifices, it was a good omen that Tlaloc would make it rain. The children were beautifully dressed and carried on platforms strewn with flowers and feathers surrounded by dancers. The children were either slaves or the second-born children of nobles.

THE 52-YEAR CYCLE

The Aztecs feared that the universe would collapse after each 52-year cycle if the gods were not strong enough. Every 52 years, a special New Fire ceremony was performed. All fires were put out for five days and, at midnight on the last day, a human sacrifice was made. The Aztecs waited for the dawn. If the sun appeared, it meant that the sacrifices for this cycle had been enough. A fire was lit on the body of a victim, and this new fire was taken to every house, city, and town. The end of the world had been postponed, at least for another 52 years!

The Aztecs had a very busy calendar! The table below shows just some of the festivals' human requirements for their 18-month year.

Aztec month	Human sacrifices
Feb 2 - Feb 21	Sacrifice of children and captives to the water gods
Feb 22 - Mar 13	Sacrifice of captives; gladiator fights; dance of the priest wearing the skin of the flayed victims
Mar 14 - Apr 2	Extraction of the heart. Burying of flayed human skins. Sacrifices of children
Apr 3 - Apr 22	Sacrifice of a maid, a boy, and a girl
Apr 23 - May 12	Sacrifice of captives by extraction of the heart
May 13 - June 1	Sacrifice by drowning and extraction of the heart
June 2 - July 21	Sacrifice by extraction of the heart
June 22 - July 11	Sacrifice of a decapitated woman and heart extraction
July 12 - July 31	Sacrifice by starvation in a cave or temple
Aug 1 - Aug 20	Sacrifices by burning to the fire gods
Aug 21 - Sep 9	Sacrifice of a decapitated and skinned woman with a young man wearing her skin; sacrifice of captives by hurling from a height and extraction of the heart

Ordeal by Fire

The Aztecs often used burning as a method of sacrifice. To appease Huehueteotl (pictured right), the fire god, the Aztecs would prepare a large feast, after which they would burn captives. Before the victims died, they would be taken from the fire and their hearts would be cut out. The Aztecs believed that if they did not please Huehueteotl a plague of fire would strike their city.

Wicker man festivals are still held today but obviously no one is sacrificed!

Burning a wicker man is an ancient pagan ritual mostly seen in Great Britain and done on May 1st, the pagan start of summer. The wicker figure represented the pagan sun god. In pagan times, the sun god was believed responsible for giving life or taking it away. If the community had a poor crop, pagans would sacrifice animals or people to please the gods. Compartments were built inside the wicker structure to place grain, small animals, and people as offerings to the god. The wicker man would then be set on fire. Pagans believed that to be sacrificed was an honor as your spirit would come back as the next season's crops, helping your children and ancestors survive.

Sati - A Hindu Widow's Ritual

An old Hindu custom meant a widow could be burnt to death on her dead husband's funeral pyre. Sometimes it was done voluntarily, but sometimes she would be dragged against her wish to the lighted pyre. One theory says that Sati began when a jealous queen heard that dead kings were welcomed in heaven by hundreds of beautiful women. She demanded to be burnt on her dead husband's pyre to keep an eye on him in heaven!

A widow burning on her husband's funeral pyre

REALLY?

In Viking tradition, dead chieftains would be burnt in a longboat with grave offerings and sometimes a sacrificed servant girl. She would be given alcohol to drink, and then men would beat on their shields to disguise her screams. Once she was killed, she would be placed on the longboat with the chieftain, and it would be set alight. Afterwards, a hill was built over the ashes.

The Afterlife

Many cultures believed in some kind of an afterlife. This belief often led to volunteers for sacrifices because the victims thought they would live on after death, and their sacrifice was not a permanent state. Important people would often be buried with things they would find useful in the afterlife, too. This could be a boat or some food, but it also could be their servants and advisors, killed specially to accompany their master.

When King Aha of Egypt's mummified body was buried, six people were poisoned and buried along with him to join him in the afterlife. One was a child of just four or five, perhaps the king's son or daughter. The child wore expensive ivory bracelets and tiny lapis beads. Aha's three-chambered tomb was piled with the things he would need for his life in eternity. There was meat, bread, cheese, dried figs, beer, and wine. As well as the six bodies buried with Aha, beside his tomb were 30 more graves laid out in three neat rows, presumably for loyal courtiers and servants who also joined their king in the next world.

An ancient Egyptian carving from Luxor, Egypt, showing a sacred barque boat carrying a pharoah to the afterlife

USEFUL LLAMAS

Near a fishing village in Peru, the skeletons of 42 children were discovered in a shallow grave. Alongside the children were 76 skeletons of **camelids**, most likely llamas but possibly alpacas, presumably intended to transport the victims to the afterlife. The children may have been sacrificed as part of a ritual associated with the ocean.

REALLY?

One 15-year-old female Inca sacrifice was selected a year in advance. Hair logs a chemical record of what a person eats. Tests on her long hair show she was raised mostly on a **protein**-poor diet rich in potatoes up until a year before her death. Then her diet became protein-rich with maize and llama meat.

Qin Shi Huangdi, a later king of Qin, was responsible for the terracotta army.

The ancient Chinese buried slaves alive with their owners after their death as part of a funeral service. In earlier times the victims were either killed or buried alive, while later they were usually forced to commit suicide. The practice was started by Duke Wu of Qin, who had 66 people buried with him. Duke Mu had 177 people buried with him, including three senior government officials. The tomb of Duke Jing of Qin had more than 180 coffins containing the remains of 186 victims. Shaped like an upside-down pyramid, the tomb is as deep as an eight-story building and is the size of a palace. It is the largest tomb ever excavated in China.

The Mayans

The Mayans believed that the cosmos had three major planes: Earth, the underworld beneath, and the heavens above. The Mayan underworld is reached through caves and deep tunnels. The Mayans offered the gods hearts from their victims, much like the Aztecs did. Sacrifices were also made with arrows, by flaying, **decapitation**, throwing people off a great height, and throwing victims into a limestone sinkhole.

A chac-mool stone statue from the Mayan temple at Chichén Itzá. Sacrificed hearts would be placed on the tray on its stomach.

Mayan human sacrifice was performed in the hope that the gods would provide rain and a good harvest. Mayans believed that the gods had given life to mankind by sacrificing parts of their own bodies. To repay the gods, the Maya practiced **bloodletting**. This most precious fluid was the greatest gift these people could offer to the gods. Maya priests used obsidian knives, stingray spines, and knotted cords to draw blood from their own bodies as offerings to a god. The blood was collected on paper, which was burned, transferred to the gods in the rising smoke.

Mayans painted their sacrifice victims blue before heading up to the top of the pyramids.

At the Mayan temple at Chichén Itzá, there is a cenote. A cenote is a naturally formed well leading to an underground river. It was a place of human sacrifice. The victims were probably bound hand and foot, and thrown into the deep water below. Mayans believed these sinkholes to be **portals** that led into the underworld. According to their beliefs, those thrown into the sinkholes would not die. Gold, jade, pottery, and incense, as well as human remains, have been found at the cenote. While a variety of people were thrown into the cenote, young males were most commonly sacrificed, presumably because they represented strength and power.

The cenote at Chichén Itzá

Ball Games

Some societies had some pretty strange ways of selecting their sacrificial victims. The Mayans played a game in which two teams tried to hit a rubber ball through two high hoops built into walls on opposite sides of a court.

The game represented the struggle between light and dark. At the end, one team was sacrificed. While it would be most obvious to think it was the losing team, some experts think it may even have been the captain of the winning team that was sacrificed, as sacrifice was considered a privilege!

A carving from the ball court at El Tajin showing a ball player being sacrificed.

hoop

hoop

Ball court in the ancient Mayan city of Coba, Mexico

Ball courts were public spaces used for a variety of events and ritual activities like musical performances and festivals. Enclosed on two sides by stepped ramps that led to ceremonial platforms or small temples, the ball court itself was of a capital "I" shape and could be found in all but the smallest of Maya cities. In Classic Maya, the ball game was called pitz. The game was played with a ball roughly the size of a volleyball but heavier and made from rubber. Decapitation is particularly associated with the ball game, severed heads are featured in ball game art. Some people even think that the heads and skulls were used as balls.

REALLY?

The Moche Inca would choose people to sacrifice by playing a game. Two warriors would try to knock off their opponent's headdress. The loser was led with other losers in a procession to the place of sacrifice. At least one of them would be bled to death, and his blood would be offered to the gods.

WIN A CITY

The Mixtec people played a ball game which was used to resolve disputes between cities. The rulers would play the game instead of going to battle. The losing ruler would be sacrificed. The ruler "Eight Deer" was considered a great ball player and won several cities this way, until he lost a ball game and was sacrificed himself.

King Eight Deer Jaguar Claw (right)

Bizarre Sacrifices

People through history have sacrificed themselves, their sisters, or their babies. In Japan, a ritual known as "seppuku" was practiced. It was a ritual in which the warrior was required to cut himself, and then be killed. The ritual was carried out to restore family honor.

A woodblock print of a warrior about to perform seppuku

Seppuku was done as part of the honor code of the samurai warriors. It could be done **voluntarily** so that a samurai would die with honor rather than fall into the hands of their enemies. Sometimes it was a punishment for samurai who had brought shame on themselves. The ceremony was usually performed in front of spectators. A samurai was bathed, dressed in white robes, and fed his favorite meal. When he had finished, his knife was placed on his plate. The warrior would then prepare for death by writing a death poem. The samurai would plunge a short blade into the abdomen and move the blade from left to right in a slicing motion. Then he would stretch out his neck for an assistant to cut his head off with a sword. Committing seppuku at the death of one's master, known as "oibara," followed a similar ritual.

When a woman became a widow in Fiji, she was strangled. It was typically the woman's brother's duty to perform the task, or at least oversee it. Any man who failed to strangle his sister was despised by his brother-in-law's family. According to Fijian belief, at a certain place on the road to the afterlife, a terrible god called Nanggannangga waited. He did not like the ghosts of the unmarried. He was especially ruthless toward all male ghosts who came to him with no wife. He would grab them, lift them above his head, and break them in two by dashing them down on a rock.

OLMEC BABIES

At the Olmec site at El Manatí, Mexico, complete skeletons of newborn or unborn children have been discovered along with other offerings leading to speculation that the Olmecs performed infant sacrifice. No one is sure how the infants met their deaths. Several works of Olmec ritual art shows a man presenting a limp half-man half-jaguar baby, like the Las Limas figure on the right. The were-jaguar is an Olmec theme represented in many statues.

Human Foundations

If a building was proving difficult to construct, a few human sacrifices buried in the foundations would make the gods happy and bring good fortune.

The Great Wall of China is an immense structure stretching 13,171 miles (21,196 km). A labor force of soldiers, convicts, prisoners of war, and farmers were forced to build it. Legend says that if any of the labor force tried to run, the punishment was to be buried alive, and, if they died of natural causes, they were buried on the spot. Many died of starvation and disease. Thousands of bodies are said to have been buried in the foundations of the wall. Many bodies have been found buried close by, too.

REALLY?

The Great Wall of China took 1,000 years to build. It is called "the longest cemetery on earth" because so many people died building it.

The impressive Aztec city of Tenochtitlán, in the center of what is now Mexico City, was built on a shallow lake. The swampy ground caused the temples to sink, and they needed to be repaired or rebuilt several times. To stop the structures from sinking, the main temple reportedly has 80,400 human sacrifices buried at its base. This ceremony was performed to re-consecrate the building after a rebuild in 1487, and the prisoners were all killed over the course of four busy days!

A painting of how Tenochtitlán would have looked, with causeways across the lake leading to the great city

In August 2012, archaeologists discovered a mix of 1,789 human bones in Mexico City. The burials date back to the 1480s and lie at the foot of the main temple in the sacred ceremonial precinct of the Aztec capital. The bones are from children, teenagers, and adults, and a complete skeleton of a young woman was also found at the site.

Skull Racks

A skull rack is a public display of the skulls of sacrificial victims. Tenochtitlán had a wooden skull rack displaying 60,000 skulls.

A relief of a skull rack in the ruins of the Tenochtitlán temple

23

India and the Thuggees

Members of India's Thuggee sect strangled people as sacrifices to appease the bloodthirsty goddess Kali. The number of victims since the practice began in the 1500s has been estimated to be as high as 2 million. Thugs were claiming about 20,000 lives a year in the 1800s. At a trial in 1840, one Thug was accused of killing 931 people himself.

The word "Thuggee" means "deceivers." Bands of Thugs traveled in groups across the country pretending to be pilgrims, merchants, soldiers, or even royalty. Offering protection or company, they would befriend fellow travelers and slowly build their trust along the road. Often they would travel for days and hundreds of miles with their intended victims, waiting for an opportunity to strike. When their targets were relaxed, a signal would be given, and the Thugs would strike. Each member had a specialty; some distracted their quarry, some made noise or music to mask any cries, while others guarded the campsite from intruders and escapees.

A thuggee gang distracting a traveler

Thugs of the highest rank performed the actual killings. As bloodshed was not allowed, the murders were performed in a bloodless way. It was a matter of honor for the Thugs to let no one escape alive once they had been selected for death. When tackling a large group of travelers, a Thuggee band might join a group in stages, pretending not to know each other. The killing place was chosen for its remoteness. Thugs tended to develop favored places of execution, called beles.

REALLY?

The usual method was strangulation with a yellow silk handkerchief Thugs wore tied around their waists. Occasionally they would break a victim's neck or poison them.

HINDU GODDESS KALI

Two hundred years ago, a boy was killed every day as a sacrifice at the Kali temple in Calcutta. In Hindu mythology, Kali is a ferocious slayer of evil with a big appetite for blood. Thugs were mainly Hindu, but they could be Muslim, or sometimes Sikh. Many Thugs worshipped Kali and considered themselves to be children of Kali, created out of her sweat. Thugs believed their murders had a positive role, actually saving humans' lives. Without Thugs' sacred service, Kali might destroy all humankind. Nowadays most Kali temples use large pumpkins to represent a human body for sacrifice instead.

The Hindu goddess Kali with her skull necklace, her foot resting on a body

Cannibals

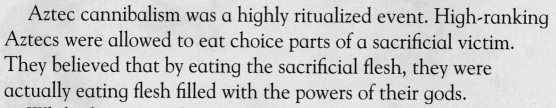

Sometimes it wasn't enough to just sacrifice your victims. Some civilizations liked to eat them too! Eating human sacrificial victims or enemies who had been killed in battle was thought to give power to the people eating them.

Aztec cannibalism was a highly ritualized event. High-ranking Aztecs were allowed to eat choice parts of a sacrificial victim. They believed that by eating the sacrificial flesh, they were actually eating flesh filled with the powers of their gods.

While there is no direct evidence that cannibalism was normally practiced in ancient Egypt, the "Pyramid Texts" carved on the walls of sarcophagi and pyramids of ancient Egypt include a section called "The Cannibal Hymn" that hints that pharoahs could gain the magical powers of the gods through eating a human sacrifice: "Pharaoh is he who eats men and lives on gods."

A drawing of an Aztec ritual: eating human sacrifices

In some tribal societies, cannibalism was frequent. Eating a person from within the same community—for example, ritual cannibalism of the recently **deceased**—can be part of the grieving process. It was also thought to be a way of guiding the souls of the dead into the bodies of living **descendants**. Eating people from outside the community was usually as a celebration of victory against a rival tribe. Eating a person's flesh or organs was believed to give the cannibal some of the characteristics of the deceased.

LEOPARD SOCIETY

In West Africa, the Leopard Society was a secret society active into the mid-1900s. The Leopard Society practiced cannibalism. Centered in Sierra Leone, Liberia, and Côte d'Ivoire, the Leopard men would dress in leopard skins, attacking travelers with sharp claw-like weapons in the form of leopards' claws and teeth. The victims' flesh would be cut from their bodies and shared out among members of the society. The ritual cannibalism was supposed to strengthen the members as well as their entire tribe.

Human Sacrifice Today

Human sacrifice is not just a ritual act designed to appease the gods. Any time a human life is exchanged for a greater cause can be called human sacrifice. Even religious belief is not a necessary requirement; hunger-strikers dying for their cause or Kamikaze pilots dying for their emperor in World War Two were both sacrifices.

Kamikaze means "divine wind." Like the samurai, the tradition of death instead of defeat was important in Japanese military culture. Kamikaze pilots would attempt to crash their aircraft into enemy targets. It was claimed that the pilots were volunteers. Ceremonies were carried out before kamikaze pilots departed on their final mission. They were given the flag of Japan or the rising sun flag, inscribed with inspirational and spiritual words. They generally drank sake, a Japanese wine, before they took off. They put on a hachimaki headband with the rising sun and a senninbari, a "belt of a thousand stitches" sewn by a thousand women who made one stitch each. They also composed and read a death poem, like the samurai tradition.

A Kamikaze plane with the rising sun symbol

REALLY?

Modern day sacrifices are different from the ritual human sacrifices of ancient people. Some people think that the executions of condemned men and women in prisons is a form of sacrifice, as it is a removal of evil which cleanses society, similar to the Aztecs killing criminals.

MEDICINE MURDERS

A medicine murder is the killing of a human being in order to take body parts to use as medicine. This practice occurred in southern Africa and is still believed to take place occasionally today. Traditional healers make medicine (or muti) which supposedly strengthens the personality of the person who orders the killing. Victims are often young children or elderly people. The victim is taken, often at night, to an isolated place and killed. The resulting medicine is sometimes eaten, but is often made into a paste that is carried by the person who ordered the killing, or rubbed onto fresh scars. As recently as 2001, a young boy's body was found in the Thames river in London, England. He was believed to have been killed in a muti ritual. A potion that contained ingredients used in West African ritual magic were discovered in his stomach.

Glossary

bloodletting
The withdrawal of blood from a person.

camelid
Any of a family of 2-toed ruminant mammals having a 3-chambered stomach and including camels, llamas, and alpaca.

decapitation
Cutting off someone's head.

descendant
A person descended from another, like a child of a parent.

deceased
Someone who has died.

famine
An extreme general shortage of food.

garrotte
An implement such as a wire with a handle at each end for strangling someone.

heretics
People who believe or teach something opposed to accepted beliefs.

intoxicating
The effect of a substance such as an alcohol so a person has reduced physical and mental control.

obsidian
A dark natural glass formed by the cooling of lava.

oxygenization
Reacting to the oxygen in the atmosphere.

portals
Passageways from one realm to the next.

protein
A substance that is essential for life, and is supplied by various foods such as meat, milk, eggs, nuts, and beans.

pyres
Heaps of wood for burning a dead body.

ritual
According to religious law or social custom.

voluntarily
Doing something of one's own free will.

For More Information
Books

Ackroyd, Peter. *Cities of Blood (Voyages Through Time)*. Dorling Kindersley Publishers Ltd, 2004.

DK Publishing, eds. *Aztec, Inca and Maya*. DK Children, 2011.

Grace, N.B. *It Came from the Swamp! Was This Mummy Murdered?* Scholastic, 2011.

Websites

Aztec Sacrifice
www.aztec-history.com/aztec-sacrifice.html
Read about the Aztecs' way of life and why they sacrificed people.

BBC Learning Zone
www.bbc.co.uk/learningzone/clips/why-did-the-aztecs-make-human-sacrifices/5102.html
Learn why the Aztecs made human sacrifices in this informative video.

Bog Bodies of the Iron Age
www.pbs.org/wgbh/nova/bog/iron-nf.html
Details of 12 of the most fascinating bog body finds.

Publisher's note to educators and parents: Our editors have carefully reviewed these websites to ensure that they are suitable for students. Many websites change frequently, however, and we cannot guarantee that a site's future contents will continue to meet our high standards of quality and educational value. Be advised that students should be closely supervised whenever they access the Internet.

Index